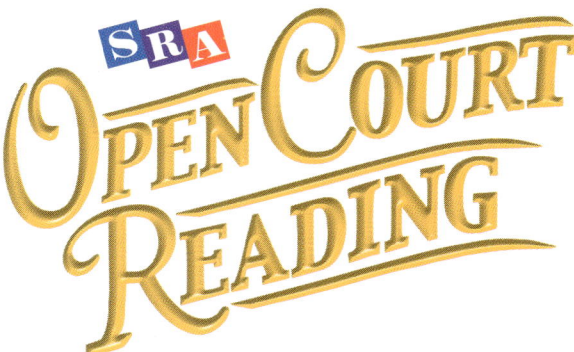

Garden Sisters

A Division of The McGraw·Hill Companies

Columbus, Ohio

www.sra4kids.com

SRA/McGraw-Hill

*A Division of The **McGraw·Hill** Companies*

Send all inquiries to:
SRA/McGraw-Hill
8787 Orion Place
Columbus, OH 43240-4027

ISBN 0-07-569481-6
1 2 3 4 5 6 7 8 9 DBH 05 04 03 02 01

This is Jennifer and her sister Amber.
Jennifer and Amber have a garden.
Jennifer and Amber are garden partners.

The sisters like plants.
Mom is a gardener.
Jennifer and Amber are Mom's
garden helpers.

"I wonder, can we plant big ferns in the garden?" asked Jennifer.
Mom said, "Yes, in the summer."

"It is winter and the garden is white,"
said Mom.

"I want to plant big ferns," Amber said.
"In the summer, I will plant big ferns."

"In the summer, Amber can plant big ferns," Mom said. "Jennifer can plant big ferns in the garden."
Jennifer and Amber felt better.
They like summer.